D0831626

Is The Cross Still There?

By George M. Bass

C.S.S. Publishing Company, Inc.
Lima, Ohio

IS THE CROSS STILL THERE?

Copyright © 1991 by
The C.S.S. Publishing Company, Inc.
Lima, Ohio

Library of Congress Cataloging-in-Publication Data

Bass, George M., 1920-
   Is the cross still there? : nine baptismal sermons / by George M. Bass
     p.   cm.
   I.SN 1-55673-279-1
   1. Baptismal sermons.   2. Lenten sermons.   3. Easter—Sermons.
4. Sermons, American.   5. Evangelical Lutheran Church in America—Sermons
6. Lutheran Church—Sermons.   I. Title
BV4277.B317   1991
252'.1—dc20
                                     90-19854
                                        CIP

9112 / ISBN 1-55673-279-1

PRINTED IN U.S.A.

For all whom I have baptized
and marked with the sign
of the cross
these sermons are dedicated
in the assurance that
the cross is still there.

Table of Contents

Introduction

This series of sermons began more than 20 years ago when an apparently stable family in our neighborhood in suburban Minneapolis started to disintegrate. Alcoholism led to the estrangement of the parents at a time when their youngest child was in confirmation class in a local Lutheran congregation. As a member of that church, I happened to be teaching that seventh grade class as part of a team of three pastors. (The pastors of the congregation were, at the time, the Rev. Paul Werger, now a bishop of the ELCA, and the Rev. Ellis Eskritt, who later became the senior pastor of the congregation.) It seemed to me that the break-up of the family, and especially the extended departure of her father from the family, hit this young girl the hardest.

It was during that turbulent year that I saw the young girl taking a photo of her father in front of their house, as if to announce to the world that her dad had returned from a 100-day absence and all was well. But it wasn't, and in a little more than a month, he left again. The marriage was ended, the family broke up, and none of the members has been the same since that time. It was a social tragedy that I was part of then and in which, with my wife, I still participate today, because the open wounds inflicted upon the members of the family continue to bleed and threaten the remaining members — the father has died — with additional pain and anguish.

Oddly enough, it is the one who was so terribly injured by the divorce whose life has taken on new meaning. She has made a good marriage, has a faithful and loving husband and two lovely children, and a satisfying career. It was my privilege to preside at her marriage and to baptize the two children, first a girl, and almost four years later, a boy. It was the baptism of the little boy, Scott, that actually gave birth to this series of sermons on baptism as an answer to the question of his four-year-old sister, Jennifer. After her brother was baptized, she asked a profound question of one of her grandmothers. She lifted the bangs on her forehead and said, "Is it (the sign of the cross) still there?" This question could not be answered in a single sermon; it demanded a fuller exploration of the biblical roots of baptism, and a set of sermons which attempt to explicate the inherent baptismal theology in terminology that would have some meaning for lay persons.

Seven of these sermons were preached in St. Luke's Lutheran Church, Bloomington, Minnesota, at the kind invitation of Pastor Ellis Eskritt. The comments of the members and the encouragement of the pastoral staff, the Rev. Richard Schowalter and the Rev. Marcia Thompson were the other pastors at that time, caused me to revise the messages and publish them. They were revised and preached the following year in St. Michael's Lutheran Church, Roseville, Minnesota, where the Rev. Roland Hayes is pastor. This manuscript represents further revision of, and additions to, the sermons that will make them suitable for preaching during Lent and Easter. They are also something of a Letter To Jennifer, who may, or may not, ever hear or read them.

These sermons are offered in the hope that they will assist pastors and their people to experience a fuller participation in Lent and Easter and the new life all share in Christ; they seek to explore some of the questions that ought to surface during Lent and Easter: Does the cross really have anything significant to say about life and death? Why is baptism so important in the worship of Lent and Easter? What does my baptism into the death and resurrection of Christ really mean? Is baptism more than an initiation ceremony into the Christian church? Does baptism really have any connection to ministry and mission? How do baptism and holy communion affirm the meaning and validity of the cross during Lent?

It is becoming more and more apparent to me that as the renewal of our baptismal covenant in our daily lives, as well as in the Easter liturgy, is the key to an in-depth celebration of the death and resurrection of our Lord. The sermons are cast in the context of Jennifer's question, "Is the cross still there? With appropriate alterations, most of the ideas, illustrations, and/or the sermons themselves, may prove to be appropriate in a sermon series for Lent and/or Easter. Perhaps, at Easter, they will help people to celebrate the reality of the cross in Jesus' resurrection, perceiving that THE CROSS IS STILL THERE on our foreheads and in our hearts, minds, and souls and will be forever!

To the pastors and people of St. Luke's Lutheran Church and St. Michael's Lutheran Church, I offer my sincere appreciation and lasting gratitude in the hope that these sermons will be of some value and inspiration to other pastors and people.

George M. Bass

August 20, 1990 — the Commemoration of St. Bernard, Abbott of Clairvaux

1
The Marked Man

"Then taking the Twelve aside he said to them, 'Now we are going up to Jerusalem, and everything that is written by the prophets about the Son of Man is to come true. For he will be handed over to the pagans and will be mocked, maltreated and spat on, and when they have scourged him they will put him to death; and on the third day he will rise again.' But they could make nothing of this; what he said was quite obscure to them, they had no idea what it means."   Luke 18:31-34

The beginning of Lent marks the start of a journey to Jerusalem. That's what it really is, although few of us will actually "go up to Jerusalem" to remember and "see" what happened there 2,000 years ago. In the environs of our congregations and communities, we will "go up" in our worship and the devotions of Lent and recall, as people who have a vital stake in a 2,000-year-old story, the events that Jesus predicted would cost him his life and, at the same time, would put the key to eternal life in the hands of all believers everywhere, in every age.

For one thing, we go up to remember that Jesus was a marked man, and to give thanks for his death. It was God's will that Jesus, his only-begotten Son, should die to save people from sin and death. When Jesus was transfigured on the mountain, God sent a specific message which made this very clear to Christ, as Luke reports the incident: "Suddenly there were two men there talking to him; they were Moses and Elijah appearing in glory, and they were speaking of his passing which he was to accomplish in Jerusalem (Luke 9:30-31)." God really does love the world so much that he gave Jesus Christ to the world — and to death — in order to do for people what they could never do for themselves. There is a cross always before us as we make this annual pilgrimage to Jerusalem. Jesus went up to Jerusalem not only to die as the prophets said he would, but to "pay the price of sin" by destroying death through his resurrection.

So he not only went up to Jerusalem to die; he went up to Jerusalem to die for us. That ought to stop us in our tracks, shouldn't it? Such knowledge should cause us to thank God for his goodness and grace, shouldn't it? Just the other day, there was a dangerous automobile accident not far from my home; a man in a pick-up truck rammed the rear of a van containing a family returning home from vacation. The collision drove the van off the highway down into a field where it overturned. The family — parents and four children — were trapped; those conscious could not free themselves. Gasoline was pouring from the fuel tank; it could explode at any moment. But a young man who works as a butcher only a mile from my home came along, stopped, investigated, and went into action. At the risk of his own life, he helped family members out of the vehicle — except for the father, who was trapped and had to be cut out of the wrecked van by the special tools of the rescue squad, so that the paramedics, who were on the scene quickly, could take over. He saved their lives by putting his own life on the line. That family will be grateful forever for what he did.

That's pretty close to the gospel story, except that one ingredient is missing: Jesus actually died for the sake and salvation of humanity, whereas the butcher risked his life, almost sacrificed his life, but fortunately did not die in the selfless action of rescuing the victims of the accident. In that regard, the butcher is much like the confessors of the early Christian church, who with the martyrs, were ready to die for the faith. They actually gave their witness to the gospel of the Lord but, for various reasons, were not executed. But Jesus made the supreme sacrifice for us. The least we — and all persons in common — owe Jesus is gratitude for his good intentions and his self-sacrifice; his suffering and death — for every one of us, believer and unbeliever alike — demands respect and appreciation. But his crucifixion also raises perplexing questions for many people: Did he really save us from sin and death by dying on a cross? Are the "claims of the cross" — forgiveness of our sins, reconciliation with God, and deliverance from death and the devil — really valid? Or is all of this just a lovely but fanciful story about a man who had strange delusions of grandeur — he claimed to be the Son of God — created by a group of deceived people?

Jesus' death on the cross would mean nothing much to us or the world and certainly would not have saved us from anything, had it not been for the fact that everything he said about his fate at Jerusalem actually occurred. Historically, we know that his enemies had him put to death on a Roman cross; there's no question that he died. And there's no doubt that he went to the cross intentionally — to save us from sin and reconcile us to God. But his death would not have been beneficial to us were it not for the fact that he rose from the dead on the third day — as he, and the prophets before him, said that he would. Jesus' cross tells us that he died to save us — and the empty tomb tries to tell us that the whole story is true, that we may believe in the cross because our Lord is alive — forever!

Every time there is a baptism that empty tomb is filled with water, the water of Easter — the water of life, as well as death. Easter tells us that the tomb has been flooded, and that every baptismal font, regardless of its size and shape, is really the vacated grave of Jesus. The font contains water which changes our lives; there is nothing accidental about this, as there was when coal mines were flooded in northeastern Pennsylvania during the Depression. My grandfather inherited a coal mine from his grandmother in the Scranton, Pennsylvania area. I remember that he was doing quite well financially when he came to live with us after my grandmother died during the early years of the Depression. He had a 1934 Ford V-8, was well-dressed, helped his son buy a home, and gave regularly and liberally to his church. But when his coal mine was flooded, the flow of money, which could have gone on for years, dried up. That, plus some poor investments, saw him ruined financially. How different his life, and that of our family, would have been, if the coal mine had not been flooded. Floods usually bring tombs of one sort or another, but when, in baptism, the tomb of Christ is flooded with water and, in effect, becomes a baptismal font, it means life to those who sink beneath the water and surface again with the "Easter Christ."

So, we go up to Jerusalem because we have a stake in what happened there, and to look into that watery "grave of life" in the hope that we will find the blessed assurance of the gospel reminding us that we belong to God, forever. In baptism, he has marked us with the sign of the cross: "_____, child of God, you have been sealed by the Holy Spirit and marked with the cross of Christ forever."[1] The water in that empty tomb has washed away the ashes of death with which we have been marked (today, in many congregations). The cross of Christ is planted in the waters of baptism, and we see reflections in the water of the font, and they are the reflections of people who have been cleansed and assured that they will live with Christ forever, and the mark of the marked man is there.

When Jennifer watched her baby brother Scott's baptism several years ago, she posed what might be the most crucial question that we should be asking at the beginning, and during Lent. Four years earlier she had been baptized at the same font, and now she stood up close, was vitally interested in everything that went on. She listened intently to the words of the baptismal liturgy; she watched the actions, especially when the water was poured on her brother's head, and as the pastor — I — traced the sign of the cross on Scott's forehead and said, "Scott, child of God, you have been sealed with the Holy Spirit and marked with the cross of Christ forever," Jennifer seemed almost mesmerized by what went on. But as soon as the liturgy was concluded, she ran over to one of her grandmothers, lifted up the bangs on her forehead, and asked her grandmother, "Is it still there?" She meant the "mark of the cross," of course.

Lent puts that important question on our lips, "Is the cross still there?" And God's word gives us an answer, which the Holy Spirit burns into our hearts, minds, and souls once again. But to hear God's "the cross is still there" and the gospel's reply, we have to go all the way to Jesus' empty, water-filled, tomb and see our reflections in it on Easter morning. That empty tomb tells us that death has been overcome by Jesus Christ, and that we don't have to worry about death anymore. Decades before people began to be concerned about "death and dying," and started to discuss death, write books and articles about the process, and teach courses on the subject in colleges, seminaries and hospitals, Dietrich Bonhoeffer wrote, in his *Letters and Papers From Prison*: "Do we not attach more importance nowadays to the act of dying than to death itself? We are much more concerned with getting over the act of dying than with being victorious over death. Socrates mastered the art of dying; Christ overcame death."

Isn't it interesting that our time has looked to Socrates' submission to a death sentence by poison for one answer to pain and hopelessness today? Death, by committing suicide, which is a procedure that the Hemlock Society supports, is becoming acceptable as a way out of this life, as a final answer to the human dilemma of pain and suffering, of life and death. God gives us different information in the cross and empty tomb of Jesus Christ! Jesus has conquered death, for everyone who believes, for every age, for all time! He has opened the way into the kingdom of heaven for each of us, as Browning declared, "A hand like this hand shall throw open the gates of new life to thee! See the Christ (the risen Christ) stand!"

So we go up to Jerusalem in the gospel story and our worship during Lent. And at the cross and tomb, we will find God's answer. Paul starts us on our way, and we declare with him: "I want to know Christ, and the power of his resurrection, and the fellowship of sharing in his suffering, becoming like him in his death so, somehow, to attain the resurrection of the dead." Jesus' "baptism" — that's what it really was — into death on that terrible tree and his glorious resurrection on the third day assure us that "The cross is still there" for each of us.

2

Marked For Death

"Remember, you are dust, and unto dust you shall return."   Genesis 3:19

"The cross is still there!" It is a reminder that all of our lives we have to live with a death sentence. We, too, are "marked people." The cross stands before us at the beginning of Lent, reasserting what God said when he passed judgment upon the whole human race in the Garden of Eden long ago: "Remember, you are dust, and unto dust you shall return." The reality of the cross is that it marks us for death, the common fate of all living creatures, of all life on earth. We are covered with "death-dust" during our pilgrimage to Jerusalem, the cross and the tomb; it has to be washed off every day, every step of the way. That dust reminds us of our mortality and God's immortality, as well as his judgment upon us as sinners. Down deep and when we face up to our sin, we know that we deserve only death and separation from him and each other, instead of life and eternal companionship in the Lord.

Dr. Robert Hughes reminds us of that in one of his sermons. Real ashes were a fact of life for him as he grew up in the coal regions of northeastern Pennsylvania; it was his task to remove the ashes from the coal-burning furnace and dump them over a bank at the rear of their home. He would be covered with ashes when the wind was blowing. Bob Hughes, writing about the "ashes of Ash Wednesday," says:

> *Not too many years ago*
> *only Roman Catholics got ashes on Ash Wednesday.*
> *I recall my confusion when I first saw the dirty*
> *   smear.*
> *Mom had a hard time explaining why it was*
> *that kids who went to St. Jerome's got ashes*
> *and kids who went to public school got nothing.*
> *It was in our seminary chapel, no more than five*
> *   years ago,*
> *that I received ashes for the first time.*
> *We came to the rail one by one*
> *where ashes mixed with olive oil were applied to*
> *   foreheads.*
> *Looking me straight in the eye Professor Krych*
> *   said,*
> *"Remember that you are dust,*
> *and to dust you shall return."*
> *Finally I had it, but I wasn't sure I wanted it.*[2]

We are all living under a sentence of death! It's as simple as that. We have been made from the dust of the earth, and in death we return to the dust once again.

The dust on our foreheads is readily washed away; a little water will do it, but — sinners that we are — we find ourselves covered with "death-dust" every day and every step of the way on our pilgrimage to Jerusalem. It is during the season of Lent that we hear the story of Jesus' death on Calvary and may begin to realize how much we have in common with our Lord; He, the very Son of God was marked for death just like we are! The difference is that Jesus' death was unwarranted;

he had done nothing to deserve death, was, in fact, obedient to the will of God "unto death."

And he wasn't allowed to die a natural death; he was executed in an excruciatingly horrible manner — nailed to a tree. His whole life was a journey to Jerusalem to be killed as a criminal. He knew that death was his destiny. Hadn't he told his disciples three times, at least, about what lay ahead of him in Jerusalem? Only much later did they understand what he had said: "The Son of Man must suffer many things, and be rejected by the elders and chief priests and scribes, and be killed, and on the third day be raised." Dr. Edmund Steimle once said: "Jesus did not just go on living after he was crucified. He died, body, soul, all of him! The final horizon had come for him just as it comes to all of us. And it is only as we face the fact that death, the last enemy, had come that Easter joy can mean anything; that God had raised him from death to life again; that the final horizon had been overcome."[3]

But where did Jesus get the spiritual resources to face such a destiny? He got them from his knowledge of God's word and the fact that God claimed him when he was baptized in the Jordan: "You are my beloved Son, in whom I am well pleased." And that's the source of the courage we need to live and the strength necessary to face the difficulties of life, particularly death.

The late and great British preacher, Dr. Leslie Weatherhead, relates an experience that he has when he attended a lecture by a brilliant scientist at Cambridge. The man opened his speech this way: "Before my lecture I want to tell you something. I am a Christian. I was brought up in a Christian home with my brother, and the two of us were the closest pals. We were both at the university together. My father and mother were deeply religious. My brother and I had no time for religion. We thought that religion was all right for old people, but we were scientists and we thought we had found our way through by what we were pleased to call scientific methods. Then my brother was killed. My father and mother had resources, and with their resources they could meet that

19

shattering loss. But I had no one. I had no resources at all. One night, broken-hearted and with all my proud science in ruined uselessness at my feet, I knelt down. I did not know how to pray. I had scorned prayer, but I put out my hand," and then in deep emotion the lecturer went on, "and I found it was grasped. I knew that someone was coming to my help and somehow I knew it was Christ. I have been a Christian ever since and no one, nothing, will take Christ from me any more."[4] Only then did he launch into his lecture.

The empty cross, which is still there, tells us that God is our help, too — in life and in death — because Jesus has participated in the total human experience. He entered into human life through his birth, and he lived it out as the Son of God, not simply by experiencing the good side of life, but by plumbing the depths of it in his death on the cross. He entered into the grave with all human beings!

One day in late October about six years ago, I went fishing on the little lake my wife and I live on. It was to be my last fishing trip of the year and it almost was my last fishing trip. About 200 yards from our dock is the deepest spot in the lake; I hooked a fish when I was over that "hole," swiveled around on my detachable boat seat to reply to a neighbor's question — he and his wife were also fishing about 100 yards away from me — "What did you catch?" As I turned, leaning back against the side of my small fishing boat, the seat came loose, and my weight tipped the edge of the boat over so far that it began to take on water. My feet were up in the air and, before I knew it, water was rushing into the boat, and I went over backward in 40-plus feet of water; the water temperature was in the low 40° range and soon penetrated the heavy clothing I had on. I was almost surprised to pop up to the surface, and I saw that the oars had come loose and were floating away, my fishing tackle box, too. I managed to get to the boat and tried to get back into it, but that only allowed more water to flow into it. I yelled to my neighbors, "I need help" and they heard me. Later, my neighbor said, "When you called to me, your boat looked like a submarine diving under the surface of the sea." My heavy clothing, in the cold water of that late fall day in Minnesota seemed to be dragging me down, and I could have suffered hypothermia and possibly, drowning, if my neighbors had not been there.

But my friends responded to my cry for help when they saw my plight, that there was no way I could get back into the boat and make my way to the shore. The man shouted, "Hang on! We're coming." He and his wife paddled over in their canoe, began to tow the rowboat toward shore. Before I could stop him, he jumped into the cold water without thinking about its temperature or depth, to help me out of the lake and on to dry land. He didn't really have to jump into the water, but he did, and that action will always be symbolic — to me — of Jesus' entrance into our death on the cross. That was the only way that he would save us — by dying as all humans die, by spending three days in the tomb, and by rising from the grave on the third day. That's why baptism is valid. His death has destroyed the permanent hold that death has had on all people.

The cross is the sign of a death sentence — Jesus' and ours — but the empty cross is also the sign through Jesus' resurrection that God has lifted the death sentence pronounced upon humanity in the garden. Baptism is a sign of life, of participating in the resurrection of Jesus Christ. Some time ago, Neville Clark wrote, "It is in baptism that the resurrection really is ever and anew proclaimed. Here the Easter event is made contemporary and visible. Here the earth trembles, and the stone is rolled away, as the power of the new age moves decisively forward in the work of recreation. For the baptized man has put on Christ, has been reclothed in his risen life, has been drawn across the chasm and given the freedom of the new world. Passed from death to life, brought back into union with the living Christ, he is inserted in the Resurrection Body of the Lord."[5]

That knowledge is of vital importance to us, not only in the face of the death sentence imposed on us and all people in the garden — "dust to dust" — but so that as we are freed from the fear of death we may, as saints as well as sinners, repent of our sins, be forgiven every day, and lead the good and godly life, the new life in Christ which is ours in baptism. The cross reminds us that we are marked for death, but it also assures us that we have God's guarantee in Jesus Christ that "the sting of death" has been extracted in Jesus' death and resurrection. Lent tells us that we are death-marked people, but Easter asures us that the cross also means life and that through baptism we participate in what happened to Jesus at Golgotha and in another garden. It was in a garden that the death sentence was pronounced upon all human beings, and it was in a garden outside of Jerusalem that it was lifted with the announcement, "He is not here, but is risen, as he said!" "The cross of the crucified and 'crowned' Christ is still there."

3

Marked By The Cross

"You have been taught that when we were baptised in Christ Jesus we were baptised in his death; in other words, when we were baptised we went into the tomb with him and joined him in death, so that as Christ was raised from the dead by the Father's glory, we, too, might live a new life." (Note: Romans 6:1-11 is really the key text for the entire sermon series.)

Romans 6:2-4

When Jennifer asked her grandmother, "Is it (the cross) still there?" I didn't hear her reply to the four-year-old girl. But since she is a Christian, active in her parish and informed about the Christian faith, I believe that she gave a positive answer, "Yes, Jennifer, the cross is still there" or something like that. She could have said, "You can't see it, but it is still there and it will always be there. You have been marked by the cross forever." She would be right on both counts, of course.

23

For one thing, the cross of Christ — the sign of God's new covenant with us in Jesus Christ — is invisible. It cannot be seen with the naked eye; it was traced on our foreheads with a "bare" finger, or possibly with water or oil. It could not be seen at all, or not for very long, at best. The "mark" of the cross in baptism is not meant to be visible in the manner that the branding of cattle or other animals is intended so that they might be identified when the visible brand is seen. One of the *National Geographic* specials on television related the story of a study made of polar bears to learn how they are coping with the infringement of modern culture upon their environment. The hunter/scientists making the study used a helicopter to locate and anesthetize a large polar bear; they shot a "loaded" dart into the animal, waited until the bear was helpless on the snow and ice, and conducted their examination. They measured the bear, checked its teeth, took blood samples, and fitted it with a tracking collar, taking great care to allow for the seasonal weight gain that occurs in these animals during the summer. The last thing they did was spray-paint on the animal a large number 25 which was highly visible from the air, as they watched the animal regain its feet and run away. In contrast, the mark of the cross, God's covenant with us, is invisible and can never be seen with the naked eye.

It is quite possible that, in a relatively short time, depending on the type of paint used to "brand" the polar bear, that mark would become invisible; it might simply be worn off. In college, I joined a fraternity in the days when hazing was still in vogue; initiation involved many of the typical pranks done in those days — taking the "pledges" out into the country, stripping them of most of their clothing and making them find their way back to town on their own, for example. But the unique part of the initiation rite of this fraternity was that the new members were actually branded with the letters of the fraternity which, they were told, would mark them for the rest of their lives. The procedure was that the person being initiated would be placed on his back after his shirt and undershirt had been removed; four "brothers" would hold him down while a stencil was placed on his chest, alcohol put in the cut out letters and ignited! The burn would heal quickly enough, if it did not become infected and it would be visible if only for a relatively short time; most of the "burns" were not too deep, so they disappeared after awhile. My brand is invisible, just as invisible as the sign of the cross that was (or should have been) traced on my forehead when I was baptized. The mark of the cross is still there on the foreheads of those who are baptized as a sign of death and new life in Jesus Christ, but it is and always will be invisible.

But the mark of the cross is also indelible. It is something like the "invisible ink" that children used to manufacture with their chemistry sets. It is indelible despite the fact that it has always been invisible because the death of Jesus Christ has burned it into our minds and souls. My "fraternity brand" faded away long ago, but the memory of that "branding" is indelible. The "cross-mark" of baptism — the invisible sign of an execution that took place in public — is indelible, because it is the mark of Jesus' suffering and sacrifice for the salvation of all people for all time. It is not simply a symbol of an abstraction; it is the sign that a man, Jesus, the very Son of God, actually was crucified outside the walls of Jerusalem. It is, to those who know and believe the gospel story, a sign that is traced in blood and can never be eradicated from the hearts and minds of those who believe that Jesus is the living Lord because the Holy Spirit has "sealed us" into a permanent relationship with the Lord.

Barbara Schmick, a liturgist who is associated with the Notre Dame Center for Pastoral Liturgy, and is also the mother of three children, tells how her three-year-old son became aware of crucifixes. He would stop, look at one, and declare, "Jesus is dead." She realized, after awhile, that he was making a "request," and was really seeking information, so she told him, "Yes, Jesus did die on a cross, but he rose from the dead. He is alive and with us still." This "sort of exchange went on for some time" and, then, one day he saw "a large outdoor crucifix" and said, 'That Jesus is dead.' " Schmich continues,

"Not knowing what to say any more and feeling a certain embarrassment at the poverty of our representations of the paschal mystery, . . . responded only, 'Yes, he looks dead.' " She says that "he took my face in his hands and looked straight into my eyes, his own wide with sudden realization. He spoke in a hushed voice as if telling me a secret, 'Maybe they don't know he's alive.' "[6] That is why it is indelible; God burns the cross into our consciousness through the good news of Jesus' resurrection. The "mark of the cross" is "still there," as it was when we were baptized. His death and resurrection have made it indelible.

So, many initiated and informed people make the sign of the cross, retracing it on themselves, with water from holy water "stoops" or baptismal fonts when they enter Christian churches, as well as at various places in the worship service. Both chapels of Luther Northwestern Seminary have baptismal fonts inside the main entrances; both were planned to complement the size of the chapels. The font in the Chapel of the Incarnation is much larger than the font in the Chapel of the Cross. But both remind the people who enter the buildings that they were marked by the cross of Christ, invisibly and indelibly, when they were baptized.

A visitor asked me, on one occasion — and I suspect that his question often goes unasked by visitors — "Why does a theological seminary need a baptismal font? It is never used, is it?" My answer was that it really is used for baptisms, on occasion, when children of students and other persons may be baptized. But the fonts need to be there not only so that the liturgical appointments of the chapels will be complete, but to remind worshipers that they have been "marked with the cross of Christ forever," that they belong to God, and that what happens between the walls of our churches, as well as in the world, is his business. That's why the font is used by some people every day; many persons (students, staff, faculty, and others) dip their fingers into the water and retrace the sign of the cross on their foreheads, because they remember their baptism into Jesus' death and his resurrection. The mark of the cross is indelible; it cannot be washed away or removed by time because the very spirit of the risen Lord makes it indelible.

One other thing must be said about the sign of the cross that "marks us" in baptism; it is an illuminated cross. In a way, it is like the church where I grew up; it had an illuminated cross on the altar, constructed with a metal "frame-outline" that held white glass in place. Light bulbs inside the cross were responsible for illuminating it as a sign and message to all who worshiped there. It said two things to the members of that congregation every time they attended a worship service: 1, Jesus, in his death and resurrection became the true Light of the world, which no one or anything can extinguish; and, 2, "Let your light so shine before others that they may see your good works and glorify your Father who is in heaven."

I have a reading lamp by my favorite chair in our den which is a constant reminder to me that the cross is illuminated by our response to the redeeming activity of God in Jesus' death and resurrection. It is an obstinate "three-way" lamp; I often turn it on and it burns properly on the highest level for a time. But, too often, it will begin to flicker and one of the two elements will go out, so that I might think the bulb is burned out. If I unscrew it a bit and then screw it back into the socket, it often burns brightly once again but, before long, it may go out entirely. That lamp, which I suspect that I don't fix because it is something of a parable of the Christian life, reminds me that my "illuminated cross" has a tendency to flicker and go out, and that it takes the word and the Holy Spirit to keep it burning brightly through my life and witness in the world.

Cross-marked people are expected to live Christian lives of love and service that, as their sincere response to Jesus' death and resurrection, tell the world that God loves them, and that they, too, love all people. When we live as real Christians, the cross of Christ is illuminated. It lights up so that others may know that Jesus is Lord and has made us children of God again. Most of us were baptized as babies, too, but our lives should reflect that light as long as we live. Our part of the covenant is to live the Christian life as best we can, and so light up the cross for all the world to see. That cross, illuminated by the loving and dedicated service to the people of the world, becomes a sign of new life and the hope of the world in our Lord Jesus Christ.

Yes, Christian, "the cross is still on your forehead." It always will be. God is the one who put it there, and though it is invisible, it is indelible and though it is a sign of death and darkness, it becomes what it really is, a sign of life and hope, a new covenant initiated by the God who created us in the first place. That cross is illuminated for others to see when we live out the covenant as children of God. Yes, children of God, that cross is on the head of every person who is baptized. Everyone who is baptized "in the name forever of the Father, and of the Son, and of the Holy Spirit" is marked with the cross of Christ forever." The cross is still there.

4

Marked In God's Book

"Their names are written in the book of life."
(Jerusalem Bible)   Philippians 4:1-9

"The cross is still there" upon your forehead, and because it is, it is burned into your heart, mind, and soul by the Holy Spirit assuring you that your "names are written in the Book of Life." God knows us and our names, and believers may rest assured that there is a place for them in God's eternal kingdom. God will never forget his people or their names, according to St. Paul.

One of the last things my wife and I did at the end of a sabbatical stay in Cambridge, England, five years ago, was to go out and visit the American Military Cemetery, outside of Cambridge, with a University of Maryland math professor and his wife. The professor had served in the U.S. Navy during World War II and wanted very much to see this cemetery, because there were sailors buried there as well as American soldiers and, largely flyers; he had not been in a military cemetery before this visit. The shocking thing about this or any military cemetery is the ages of the persons buried in them; they are mostly, very young men and an occasional young woman; some are not out of their "teens." For both of us and our wives, this was a sobering and nostalgic experience. This cemetery is not far from Basingbourne, also a few miles outside of Cambridge, which was a large American air base during that war. I discovered a plaque on the front of the headquarters building and took a picture of it; it reads:

> *To these gallant American Airmen who on*
> *August 12, 1944, sacrificed their lives to*
> *prevent their aircraft from crashing on*
> *our homes, the residents of Cheshunt and*
> *Waltham Cross in the country of Hertfordshire*
> *dedicate this plaque in grateful memory.*

2nd Lt. John D. Ellis	*2nd Lt. Robt. B. Cox*
S/sgt. Jay W. Gable	*T/sgt. Stanley E. Jankowski*
S/sgt. Clark Hultengrin	*T/sgt. John H. Holling*
F/O Samuel C. Stalsby	*S/sgt. Wm. C. McGinley*
S/sgt. Frank Minnick	*S/sgt. Jack O. Shaeffer*

Their names were emblazoned on that plaque because they had done a good and merciful work. Not unlike the early Christian martyrs, they had given their lives so that others literally might live. To the people of those two villages, their lives had been spared by an act of grace, reminiscent of that "graceful death" of Jesus at Golgotha. The flyers' names were inscribed on a plaque so that they would never be forgotten in these two villages in England.

The other evening I met a man who lives only three blocks from my home and who was stationed at Basingbourne and flew B-17 bombers out of that air base. He had been to that cemetery, and he had seen that plaque. He also knew about being shot out of the sky by anti-aircraft guns; it happened to him over Germany. He and his crew crash-landed in Belgium. Two of the crew had been killed by anti-aircraft fire; he and the others on the plane were severely wounded but survived. He said to me, "I have been to that cemetery twice." Without asking him, I believe I know why: the bodies of the two crew members killed on that mission had been brought back to England and were buried near the base from which they had flown their missions. I don't know their names, nor are they recorded on a plaque for the world to see, but their names are on their tombstones — and, as in most American military cemeteries, are recorded in a book for any visitor to read. And their names, I am certain, are inscribed on the heart and mind of my new acquaintance. That's something of how it is with God; the names of the faithful are known by the Lord and will never be forgotten by God, because they are written on "the book" of his heart.

Time was when children were given a new name — a baptismal name — when they were presented to God at the font. It was the name that would be "written" in the Book of Life. You don't hear much about that today, do you? It seems rather old-fashioned. Our children are "named" before they are baptized in the name of the Father, Son, and Holy Spirit. With the scientific tests that are used in prenatal care today, it is possible to tell the sex of a child before the mother gives birth. That means that the parents don't need to have two different sets of names, one male and the other female, selected before the baby is born; only one name, or names, is necessary now. A young couple, whom my wife and I know quite well, will have a baby in a couple of months; they know that it will probably be a girl, so they have been attempting to decide upon a name for the child. A couple of weeks ago, we heard that they were going to name the baby Jennifer Marie, but yesterday we learned that they had changed their minds and were attempting to agree on two new names for the baby. I wonder how many times they will change the child's name in the nearly two months before it will be born, and the baby's name will have to be recorded in official documents.

Not only have names been given in baptism, but those baptismal names given to children had to be — in many congregations — biblical names. That would create a problem today, when some of the names we give to children are rather exotic, even strange. The late Dr. George Buttrick once asked, "What's in a name?" and concluded that "they are hardly more than tags by which the mailman brings Christmas presents to our house instead of to some alien door. . . . But there was a time when names had meaning. . . . The name 'John' once meant 'gift of God,' just as Joshua (Jesus) once meant 'savior.' In times from which the book of Genesis was drawn, men believed that if they could learn the name of a god, they would possess the god's very power; for a name then meant almost a man's or a god's nature."[7] So maybe there really is something in giving our children biblical and baptismal names after all, because such names are reminders of the blessings that God gives his people in their baptism. They tell people that "the cross is still there." The names given in baptism indicate that God numbers the baptized among the very saints of heaven and earth.

And so the Church honors the saints, especially those who died as martyrs, witnessing in suffering and death to the power of God's grace. Paul was convinced — before the practice of "naming saints" was begun by the Church — that the names of the faithful are written in God's book of life, and that's one reason why they should be celebrated as genuine saints. They clung to their faith which they had received from God, not merely by human will and strength, but through the power of the Holy Spirit. Here's the amazing part of the whole business: God sustained all of the saints, and especially those, who in the face of terrible torture and agonizing death gave up the precious gift of life for the sake of Christ and the gospel. To be named for a biblical saint or a Christian martyr, at birth or baptism, is to stake a claim upon God's grace and the hope of eternal life.

Paul almost makes it sound, in the letter to the Church at Philippi that, by itself, serving the Lord is a good work that guarantees eternal life and gets one's name "written" in the "Book of Life." He praises the workers in their church, as well as Clement and the others who were part of his missionary company. Their names are "written in the book of life," Paul declares. But, according to the sum and substance of his writings, he meant that they had been saved by God's gracious gift in Jesus; their faith came from him, and they simply lived out their baptismal covenant in their Christian ministry; they were saved by their faith, and not because they had done a good work.

Not even those who have died for the faith have their names written in the book because they were martyrs "for Christ." Even, and especially, the martyrs were saved by the grace of God, and that's the reason their names are recorded in God's "book" and remembered and revered by the Christian church, usually on the date of their death as their "birth" in the everlasting kingdom of God. Our "death-day" at the baptismal font celebrates our "birth" as citizens of God's eternal realm of the saints and martyrs. For them — and for us — the day of our baptism, when we were named for and claimed by God, is the day when our names were written "in the book."

Today we continue to name saints, confident that God has written their names in the Book of Life but with a difference; most of the martyr-saints tend to be secularized by setting aside the day of their physical birth as their "day." That happened with the national holiday that was established for Martin Luther King Jr., to celebrate his actual birthday on January 15th; the Christian churches "commemorate" him on that day, too, instead of on the day of his death. At least, we remember how he gave his life for "liberty and justice for all" without a long and very formal process to "name" him a martyr-saint.

And Martin Luther King Jr., along wih most of the saints, will probably never be forgotten by the Church nor by God. What really matters, however, is that his name, and the names of all the saints, are written in the Book of Life that will never be destroyed. God knows our identities, loves us, and will never forget who we are. Henrietta Allen died recently and left a more than $2 million estate, which should be claimed by her heirs. But her name was never written in a book, not in a court house or church records. Her attorney cannot find a trace of her ancestry; her name is known, but there is no record of her birth, her baptism, her marriage, or anything else. It is almost as if she had never existed, or had been forgotten by the world and she would have been had she not been wealthy.[8] But, if she had been baptized, God knows her name! There is one record — God's — which will never be lost. That's God's way. He writes our names into the book of life, not the honor roll of saints named here on the earth, when we are baptized, sealed into a covenant with him, and marked with the cross of Christ forever. Our names are written there simply on the basis of what he has done, not to record our good marks or meritoriuos service.

Well, what's the point, then, of attempting to be faithful to Christ, to serve in love and mercy, as long as we live? Just this: those who know that their names are written in heaven when they are baptized, and who live good and faithful Christian lives, have the comfort of the gospel and the blessed assurance that they will be with God forever. And we know that we are loved by God whatever we do or do not do. He forgives us all our sins forever no matter what they might be when we call upon him in true repentance and faith as his children. We can live and even die with our heads held high, because God loves and forgives us.

James S. Stewart tells a story about a young girl who ran away from home. Stewart says that she "was swallowed up in a great city's shadows." Some time later, her mother set out to find her and take her home, and somehow or other, she located the girl "lonely and miserable and destitute, and brought her back" to their home. It was dark when they reached their "old home" but the girl said, "Mother, I cannot go in. I cannot face father." "But," her mother answered, "your father has been longing to see you. He has been waiting for this day, hungering to have you home." But the girl just stood there, afraid "to meet her father's gaze." "Mother," she said at last, "will you go in and turn down the lights?" And James S. Stewart adds, "And so in the darkness the reconciliation was effected."[9]

34

That's not the way it will be for those whose names are "written in the Book of Life," because God is not like that, at all. He forgives us all our sins and he will welcome us with open arms into his everlasting kingdom; of that we can be completely confident. Our baptism tells us that our names are in the Book of Life, and that's enough for us. We can live life to the fullest with blessed assurance and hope, because the cross is still there on our foreheads and in our hearts and tells us this is so.

5
Marked For Community

"Just as a human body, though it is made up of many parts, is a single unit because all these parts, though many, make one body, so it is with Christ. In the one Spirit we were all baptized, Jews as well as Greeks, slaves as well as citizens, and one Spirit was given to all to drink." v. 17f — "Now you together are Christ's body; but each of you is a different part of it." v. 25 — ". . . but that each part may be equally concerned for all the others."
1 Corinthians 12:12-13

"The cross is still there" and it reminds us that we have become part of a very special community, one in which all of the members really care about one another's welfare and happiness. The Christian church is a caring community, a loving community, and it has been so from the beginning because it is the Body of Christ on earth. Baptism is the way we enter into that community. By the physical act of being born, we join the common race of humanity; by baptism, we are made members of the Body of Christ, the church, which God has shaped into a very special community indeed. This is something that we should remember every time we see and think about the cross of Christ. The cross is the sign and symbol of that special community. God means it to be just that; surely, it was that way when the church was young and when unbelievers noticed "how these Christians love one another."

The rite of baptism has the shape of an old formula that might have been used in some sort of initiation ceremony, doesn't it? Of course, that's what a baptism is — an initiation into the Body of Christ, not simply the guarantee of the forgiveness of our sins and deliverance from death and the Devil. Through holy baptism we are admitted to membership, full membership, in the Holy Catholic Church; baptism is the only way to gain admittance to this body; there's no other way to become a member of the Christian family. That's why all of us ought to know the date, as well as the place, of our baptism so that the anniversary of one's baptism might be celebrated annually, but not just at home around the dinner table; perhaps it ought to be celebrated in the Sunday gathering of the body of Christ. Possibly once a month all baptismal anniversaries could be listed, remembered, and some sort of a celebration, maybe nothing more than the lighting of the Paschal candle and a prayer, be arranged to acknowledge them.

Three decades ago, my wife and I were sponsors for the baptism of her nephew. This was a very special baptism, because the boy, Greg, had been adopted by my wife's sister and her husband. He had been made part of their family by a legal process, and at the font, he became a member of a larger, a world-wide, family through water, word, and Holy Spirit. Greg was a toddler when he was adopted and baptized, a bit restless as I held him. In the middle of the baptismal ceremony, he suddenly grabbed a handkerchief out of my coat pocket and threw it right into the baptismal font. We laughed silently, and I quickly fished it out and held it and the baptism was completed without any other unusual occurrences. I realize now that I should have had a cross marked, or sewn, on that hand-kerchief and that I should have given it to him as a token of his baptism, his initiation into the family of God, the Church of Jesus Christ the Lord. That handkerchief is a symbol to me, too, because, unlike the paper towel in the television com-mercials, which soaks up an inordinate amount of liquid, the handkerchief could not "dry up" the water in the font. It al-ways will say to me, the water is still there. The font cannot be dried up! We enter the church by water and the word. The cross is still there.

The Christian church is a peculiar community because it is the community of the redeemed, of people whose sins have been forgiven, and people who really believe that God loves them and has really delivered them from death and the devil through the sacrifice of Jesus Christ. That's partly what makes us Christians different; we know whose we are and why. We are all in the same spiritual ship, the same boat, if you will, and for that reason, we live as people who have hope for the future, as well as for the present, in and through Jesus Christ, as well as people who really care for one another. The church is the community of the hopeful.

Just the other day, the media reported on the 90th birth-day of the Queen Mother of Great Britain. The television cover-age reminded me of one of the last things my wife and I watched toward the end of our sabbatical in Cambridge, England, a few years ago, the celebration of the 60th anniver-sary of the birth of Queen Elizabeth II at Buckingham Palace. On both occasions, the gates of the palace were opened and thousands of people were allowed to enter the grounds, present flowers to the two queens, and sing "Happy Birthday" to the two ladies as part of the birthday celebrations. We had never seen so many daffodils as on Queen Elizabeth II's birthday; she was almost overwhelmed by flowers; the Queen Mother also received flowers from her admirers and subjects. Both oc-casions were joyous events, an outpouring of real love and af-fection by the people.

But one occurrence made a real difference between the two celebrations; it happened at Queen Elizabeth II's birthday as a television camera zoomed in on one very young couple with a baby; they were punkers with multi-colored, spiked hair. A television reporter interviewed them, asking them why they were there, and the man replied, "We just wanted to see what was going on." They were curious observers, not really part of the birthday celebration. The young woman said nothing, but her head was partly shaved and the camera focused in on what was emblazoned on it: "no future." If they had made a placard to protest their estate in life, declaring "no hope," the scene would have been complete. Theirs was a sort of silent protest, perhaps, but even more of an unrecognized need to know, worship, and love the King of kings, and to know the love the members of his body, the church, have for one another. Perhaps, then, they would remove the "no future" statement from her shaved and shorn head. Love and hope go hand in hand in the community of believers, the redeemed, the hopeful.

The church remains the hopeful community, and because it is that, its members are freed up to love one another and the world. Admittedly, the church doesn't always seem to be what it is supposed to be. We have all sorts of squabbles and petty disagreements with one another, and sometimes we seem to be subjects of Satan, working to destroy hope and love, rather than disciples of Christ who are about the business of developing peace and harmony here on earth. This is especially true whenever we dare to think we are better than other people in our congregations, or even than those who reside on the streets and in the communities where we live most of the week.

My wife and I live in a neighborhood that has two or three neighborhood parties a year; we sort of rotate in hosting these events, except for a couple of families who come but never entertain. I think those families must think that they don't really belong to the neighborhood, that their welcome is more of a courtesy than a sign of acceptance as members of the community neighborhood; this may be so for various reasons. But in one case, the people are ultra-conservative Christians, who give the rest of the people the impression — whether it is true or not — that they count themselves better Christians (and every family on the street, 16 in all, is active in a church, all sorts of churches) than the rest of us. Exclusivism comes from spiritual pride, which is one of the worst sins of which we can be guilty. It reduces the community of the hopeful into people who may despise others, who may even begin to wonder about the reality of God's love. When there is no hope or love, can the cross still be there?

At the head of this street on which I live there is a sign that warns drivers — dead end. Most of the time, this is a one-block community that is anything but a "dead end" street. It is almost a microcosm of what the church should be. Beyond the occasional parties on the street, there is continuing and continual evidence that the people have something special going for them in their relationships with each other. They are friendly, good friends as well as neighbors. They help one another when there is illness or difficulty or tragedy. They are concerned in times of crises and offer the kinds of support and help one used to expect to find in a small town. It has taken time for this 16-family street to become a neighborhood, resembling what the church really is and something of how Christians ought to live with one another in care and concern and compassion. Could it be because practically all of the people are active members of different parts of the Holy Catholic Church. I like to think so. I like to think that the cross is there.

But our business, as Christians, is to love and care for all people, those outside the church, as well as those who belong to the community of Jesus Christ. To declare faith and love in him requires faithful people to live the way he did, selflessly loving others, really caring for them, and serving them regardless of the cost. The cross — not a "dollar" sign — is the symbol of the Christian community, and it is a sign of genuine love for Christ and the people of our world. To fail to love, as we have been loved by Jesus Christ, is tragic. James Russell Lowell understood this and said:

> *That love for one from which there doth not spring*
> *Wide love for all is but a worthless thing.*

Baptism is an initiation into the Christian faith, no mistake about that, but it is admittance to the Body of Christ, a caring and hopeful community, in which we are all called to entrust our lives to God and to love each other as we have been loved as well as to allow loving actions to move beyond the bounds of our community and touch those outside by our love, so that they, too, may know that they are loved by the Church, the Body of Jesus Christ. The very existence of the church as the caring community and hopeful Body of Christ tells the whole world that "the cross is still there."

6

Marked For Ministry

"We do nothing that people might object to, so as not to bring discredit on our function as God's servants. Instead, we prove we are servants of God . . . ."   2 Corinthians 6:3-4a

"He said, therefore, to the crowds who came to be baptised by him, 'Brood of vipers, who warned you to flee from the retribution that is coming? But if you are repentant, produce the appropriate fruits . . . ."   Luke 3:7-8a

The congregation of which I am a member encourages its members to celebrate their baptismal anniversaries every year by presenting those who are baptized with a small baptismal banner and a candle. The banner has the name of the person embroidered upon it, along with ". . . child of God, you have been sealed by the Holy Spirit and marked with the cross of Christ forever." The candle is to be lighted every year to remind people that they belong to Christ and his Body, and that they are "to let their light so shine before others that they may see their good works and glorify their Father in heaven." It is really an "ordination" candle, because that's really what happens to us when we are baptized. The light that shines through out witness to the gospel, our ministry, if you will, declares that the cross is still there.

You see, all of us are "ordained" in baptism into some area of ministry of the Christian church. When we are initiated into the church, the caring community, through holy baptism, we are also being ordained into the ministry of serving and witnessing in the name of Jesus Christ our Lord. Do you remember the end of the baptismal service? The baptismal liturgies of most churches have something like this that is read toward the end of the rite: "Through baptism God has made these new sisters and brothers members of the priesthood we all share in Jesus Christ." Do you think of yourself as being a priest of Jesus Christ? Probably not, although the priesthood of all believers is a cardinal doctrine of the Lutheran church and some other churches. Priesthood is more than having direct access to God in prayer; it is also the discharge of ministerial responsibilities by the faith.

Ministry is a matter of response, commitment, and self-sacrifice. Jesus — now as then — gathered disciples around himself, calling for complete commitment in terms of "the cross": "If any man (woman) would come after me, let him (her) deny himself (herself), take up his (her) cross, and follow me." The last statement of the baptismal service (Lutheran) affirms that we, as Christians, are "following" Jesus, and we, therefore, invite the newly baptized to join us in our ministry: "We welcome you into the Lord's family. We receive you as fellow members of the body of Christ, children of the same heavenly Father, and workers with us in the kingdom of God." The exhortation in *The Book of Common Prayer* makes the "work" of the baptized most specific, a clear command: "We receive you into the household of God. Confess the faith of Christ crucified, proclaim his resurrection, and share with us in his eternal priesthood." Jesus Christ calls us to follow him, to work in his kingdom, that is, to live out the Christian faith in the world, and he ordains us for that work in holy baptism.

From one perspective, this means that we will engage in the "obvious" activities generally associated with the Christian faith — evangelism, works of mercy, world missions, stewardship — but these activities will have to be done in a new manner in a radically changing world. Therefore, stewardship will have to assume new meaning and new directions; it cannot mean simply going to the church at home or abroad, to the support of ecumenical activities, or even to the poor and needy today, although such activities need to be continued. The care of the earth becomes basic for Christian stewards, who hear God's voice from the garden telling people to "care for the earth and fill it up." Real environmental concerns make us aware of the importance of this kind of basic stewardship. Time may be running out on all life here on the earth! Something has to be done now!

"Canary In A Coal Mine" is the title of an article researched and written by Karin Winegar, a staff reporter for the Minneapolis *Star Tribune*. It isn't about a canary, nor is it about a coal mine; it is about a woman, Cindy Froeschle Duehring, who is living like a "canary in a coal mine." She is dying from "environmental illness" (EI), which "is not something you are born with; you get it from the 20th century." It is also known as "multiple chemical sensitivity (MCS) or total allergy syndrome or chemical hypersensitivity." Most people who have it don't know it; their illnesses are frequently misdiagnosed. Cindy is the wife of a Lutheran pastor, who lives with her husband outside Williston, North Dakota. Her illness is so acute that she can't go outside her home; she can't even look at the outside world through the windows.

Karin Winegar writes in her article about Cindy Duehring: "To survive (her illness is so bad that she goes into seizures when she is exposed to too much light, to perfume and hair spray, to gasoline fumes — almost anything else in the environment), she has retreated to a sealed, filtered house built of non-toxic materials on a remote slope in the North Dakota grasslands."[10] Sleep, diet, activities — anything she does — are all carefully monitored, but she still gets sick when she eats; she is a virtual prisoner — "a canary in a coal mine" — who is amazingly cheerful and "up" most of the time. She is a symbol of what is occurring in our world and may happen to all life if we do not really "care for the earth."

Two things are evident: One, we are all "canaries in a coal mine" and, like Cindy Duehring, we must face that reality. The world is closing in on us. Our environment will destroy us sooner or later; we all live with the threat of the EI "virus," environmental illness. But unlike Cindy who was "innocently" poisoned by pesticides, we have brought this possible malady — unintentionally, of course — on ourselves. And two, she is doing everything she can to cope with and conquer her illness. And that's a sign of the direction in which people have to go in their basic stewardship of the earth, if they want to survive in the world. It is a matter not simply of protecting ourselves from the environment, but of protecting it, doing all we can to preserve it, and the resources of the earth.

Another writer, Connie Koenenn, suggests the "Top 10 simple steps to save the Earth:"

1. Turn down your water heater (to 130°).
2. Put a plastic bottle in your toilet tank.
3. Install low-flow faucet aerators and shower heads.
4. Keep your car's tires properly inflated.
5. Bring your own shopping bag (to the store).
6. Eliminate waste before you buy.
7. Recycle cans, glass and paper.
8. Replace a regular (incandescent) light bulb with a compact fluorescent light bulb.
9. Buy rechargeable batteries for household use.
10. Set the blades higher on your lawn mower.[11]

These suggestions are at least a beginning and really will make a difference, if people care enough to take such measures in "saving" the earth.

The waters of baptism, through us and our "care of the earth," can wash clean the face of the earth again so that it remains hospitable to all life. Because the cross is still there, it reminds us that this is basic business of our ordination, and that it belongs to the work of the kingdom of God. As ministers and priests of Christ, we have to save the earth as well as participate in saving the people who live on it.

God not only calls us to work in the kingdom, but he gives us gifts for service, all kinds of gifts, so that the work of the kingdom can be done here on earth. The church is made of ministers, many of them, who are given abilities that will be useful to the upbuilding of the church in the world. The work that gifted people do, in the name of the Lord, is just as important as the ministry of the pastors of the church. A theological seminary is a mother lode of these gifts. Every seminary has students who have extraordinary, as well as ordinary, gifts for ministry — in this case, the ministry of the word and sacraments. God calls all sorts of people to full-time ministry — young and more mature persons, scholars and scientists, mathematicians and mechanics, poets and police persons, musicians and magicians, teachers and truck drivers, pilots and painters. God gives people gifts for ministry, not only in word and sacraments, but in caring for people and the world and by doing so testifying and witnessing to the grace and goodness of Christ. It is our responsibility to discover these gifts and to use them in the work of the church in the world.

We had a pastor on our staff at the seminary a couple of years ago who resigns his parish every 10 years and engages in a different type of ministry for a year as a kind of educational sabbatical leave. He worked in our contextual education department, which supervises students as they do field work in parishes and in their intern year, the third year of the four-year course of study at the seminary. He was with us only that one year, because he filled the position of a person who was on a year's leave and returned in the fall. "Shortly," he told me during the spring, "I will begin looking for a call to a congregation; I love parish ministry. But I want to go to a congregation where all the members know that they are ordained priests and are actively serving Jesus Christ in his church.'' He said, ''When I interview with a committee and church council, I will ask them how they have functioned during their pastoral vacancy. If they have been actively serving Christ and been effective in their ministry, I will ask them if they are willing to continue to work and serve as they did during the vacancy. I want to spend as much time as I can doing the specific things a pastor must do — preaching and teaching, calling, studying, counseling, visiting the sick and administering the sacraments, bringing comfort to those who hurt. I want to spend as little time and energy as possible in administration, in attending meetings, or otherwise doing the things that the people have been doing while they had no pastor. That's the sort of parish I'm looking for,'' he declared. More importantly, that is the sort of parish that Christ is looking for, a parish that knows the meaning of baptism as the ordination of all, and goes about responding to God's grace by producing the ''fruits of righteousness,'' actively engaging in God's work — all of it — here on the earth.

To fulfill our baptismal covenant means that we will recognize our ordination into the ministry of Jesus Christ here on earth is a privilege, not a burden, and that it is what we do every day, full-time ministry. Ministry is really a way of life, not only for the relatively few persons who are called and ordained to the ministry of word and sacrament, but for all Christians. Baptismal ordination calls for a lifestyle that tells the world that we belong to God and to Christ and his Body, the church, here on earth. Therefore, all baptized Christians are ordained ministers, ordained to serve God and people — deliberately and positively — and to do all of the work that God has given us to do as good stewards here on earth — in the name of Jesus Christ.

It would be well if all of us would celebrate our baptismal anniversary every year, and come to celebrate it as an anniversary of our ordinations . . . and then do our best to serve and witness to Christ every day of our lives. The cross is still there, and it is a symbol of our ordination, of who we are and what we are to do in the world in the name of Jesus Christ our Lord. It means that we all have been marked for ministry here on earth.

7

Marked For Mission

"Go out to the whole world; proclaim the Good News to all creation. He who believes and is baptized will be saved; he who does not believe will be condemned."   Mark 16:14-20

Yes, "the cross is still there, and that means that we are all responsible for the business of telling the story of Jesus to the world. Shortly before it actually occurred, Jesus spoke of his impending death on the cross, ending with, "And I, if I be lifted up, will draw all people to myself." After his resurrection and just before he ascended to be with the Father, his last words were, "Go out to the whole world; proclaim the Good News to all creation." The gospel has to be communicated to people before they can believe that Jesus Christ is Lord and that "the cross is there" for them. Mission is basic to the business of Christian ministry.

It is certainly true that this command was given to the apostles originally, but we are all called to be witnesses to the

Christian faith by reason of our baptism. Listen to a Roman Catholic New Testament and liturgical scholar, Father Gerard Sloyan: "With you . . . there is the reiterated pledge of fidelity to the promises of your infancy, or whenever you were baptized. You intensify the life of the baptized by giving a fresh and explicit testimony to your faith in Christ. You declare yourselves martyrs, witnesses." And he declares, "A risen life is the best testimony to the resurrection of our Lord, in whom we live."[12]

All of us who believe in Christ are involved in Christ's mission of mercy and service. We are to do the things that our Lord did, not to gain salvation but as a loving response to his love and mercy in his death and resurrection. And people sometimes — not always, I am persuaded — find Christ in the good that is done on their behalf. For some people, works of mercy and, especially, miracles performed in the name of Christ are the most positive way that Jesus makes himself known in the world. But in the history of the church, the testimony of miracles has been more of an in-house, or in-church, type of phenomenon that may have more negative than positive implications for the faith than a means of proclaiming the gospel to the world. The most positive way to help people encounter the living Lord is through the telling of the story, the gospel of our Lord, by word and then, by deed.

We not only serve, but we also, as baptized members of the Body of Christ, are expected to give specific and public testimony to the faith given us by God in Christ Jesus our Lord, as you have heard again and again in Sunday School, first, and in church, too. We tend to call our witnessing in our communities evangelism, but I'm afraid that is often a matter of inviting people to join our church more than it is actually evangelizing them with the good news in Jesus Christ. We assume that they already know about Jesus, his death and resurrection, and that all we have to do is tell them about our congregation and perhaps sell them on why they should be part of it. That may be okay, but if you want to see what real evangelism does, genuine witnessing to the gospel of Christ, go to Africa or China.

My wife and I went to China a couple of years before the massacre in Tianamen Square. It was a most interesting experience, but the most interesting part of it was in the dynamics between the tour guides. Our group had two American tour guides, both of whom were ordained pastors. One, the Rev. Anders Hanson, had been born in China and had served as a missionary in China until he was expelled as a young man. He went to Hong Kong with his wife and sister, who were also born in China, and the three of them witnessed to the faith for some three and a half decades in Hong Kong. The other tour guide was a retired pastor — the Rev. Luther Anderson, Pastor Hanson's brother-in-law. In addition, two Chinese women were assigned to travel with our group for almost three weeks, and additional local guides supplemented their leadership in the major cities we visited.

It was the witness, the missionary activity, of the American tour guides, especially that of Pastor Hanson, that was most intriguing. Neither Chinese guide had been to a Christian worship service; they had never heard the gospel, and when they did hear the good news about Jesus they were curious, if not captivated, by it. They asked questions and received answers, were given copies of the Bible and Luther's *Small Catechism*. When they were offered a cash gratuity at the end of the tour, they asked — of course, they weren't supposed to take "tips," — that it be given to the Shanghai Community Church, where they first heard the gospel, "in their names." Before they were baptized, they already were busy with, and participating in, the work of the kingdom, the work of the baptized, witnessing to the gospel of Jesus Christ.

Baptism involves us in the business of taking the gospel to all people in the world; God's will is that every person should have a chance to hear the story of Jesus Christ and the opportunity to believe and be baptized as we have been. Some people will actually go to the four corners of the earth to preach and teach people the good news. That task never gets finished; every age demands that missionaries be sent to fulfill Jesus' command. Some time ago, there was an article in the Minneapolis *Star Tribune* titled, "Bishop says Christianity is growing in Africa." The bishop is Abel Muzorema, former prime minister of Zimbabwe, the country that used to be known as Rhodesia; Bishop Muzorema was one of the leaders in the movement to attain self-rule for that country. He says that more than six million people are converted to the Christian faith every year in the entire continent of Africa. The Methodist Church, which he serves, grows at about a 20 percent rate annually.

Bishop Muzorema elaborates, "Even before the missionaries our people believed that people who died only departed from their physical lives, and we always took our petitions through our ancestors to the creator of all people. We knew God, we just didn't know Jesus. Then we were told how he died and was resurrected. That makes a lot of fire (or faith) in people."[13] One of my colleagues, Dr. Lee Snook, recently spent two years teaching in the university in the capitol of Zimbabwe; his missionary activity was in his teaching ministry. The native sculptures, which he brought back with him, gave evidence of the impact of the gospel on the people of that part of Africa. They have heard the good news and have received it for what it is: the story of God's love for all people in and through Jesus Christ and his cross. They are coming to know Jesus Christ as Lord. But remember, there are still people who have not heard the story, and missionaries, as preachers and teachers, will be needed until the end of time and the Lord makes his promised return.

Baptism involves us all in this, some as missionaries, the rest learning about and supporting the work of missions. The son of our next-door neighbors, John Lewis, is a missionary pilot in Zaire, Africa; he and his wife have been there over eight years. He is in charge of flying mercy missions which transport people to the main mission hospital. They have recently returned home for a short furlough; they return to Africa in December. You wouldn't believe the price they have paid to be missionaries — mission money stolen by their houseboy, a near-death experience on a river, malaria and other health problems.

A couple of years ago, John had to return to mission headquarters in California; he brought his daughter with him for diagnostic testing and treatment at a California hospital. She had a kidney infection which could not be cleared up in Africa; while she was in the hospital, her malaria flared up. She was so ill that her mother had to be flown in with her younger brother, whose rare type of malaria had also become acute in the meantime. All four of them paid a tremendous price to engage in missionary work in Zaire, Africa. When Anita, John's wife, became pregnant with her third child, her pregnancy became so complicated that she had to be returned to the United States; her very life, let alone that of the child in her womb, was at stake. A physician had to accompany her on the trip. She and the baby both survived and she took the young child back to Africa with her as soon as she had recovered. Because they and other Christians are faithful witnesses to the gospel, the cross is there, still there.

I don't tell you that story, and there are others like it that I could, maybe should, relate to you, to make you feel guilty or ashamed, but simply to show how God gives his grace abundantly to those who respond to his command and follow the Lord from the cross and empty tomb into all the world, preaching the good news as they go. It is essential that we learn about world missions, that we pray for them, and that we support them financially, but it is also necessary that some people actually go "into all the world" to preach, teach and baptize in the name of Jesus Christ.

In the neighborhood where we lived before moving to our present home, we lived across the street from a physician who was serving a residency in surgery. He and his wife had five children: two boys and three girls; it was a lovely and devoted family, whose members were very much involved with their church. They moved to California after he completed his residency and, potentially, "they had it made." Their lifestyle could have been anything they wanted it to be, but they have continued to be involved in the work of the church and of missions. Gradually, all five of the children have become missionaries — either medical (one boy is a surgeon, one girl is a nurse) or educational missionaries in various parts of the world. They seem to have taken Jesus at his word, "Go into all the world and . . ." Perhaps he will give us the grace to be involved in that work and to fulfill the mandate for mission that our baptism puts upon us. The cross is still there and it will always point us to the ends of the earth and tell us to take the gospel to every person on the earth.

So in various ways — by being concerned enough about people who haven't heard the gospel, by prayer, financial support, by learning about people and mission, and actually accepting Christ's call to go out and preach the gospel all over the world, we will be going back to Africa with my neighbors and to the ends of the earth with other missionaries and, at the same time, we will be living out our baptismal covenant made with us by our Lord, because the cross is still there.

8

Marked At The Table

" 'If I do not wash you, you can have nothing in common with me.' 'Then, Lord,' said Simon Peter, 'not only my feet, but my hands and my head as well!' Jesus said, 'no one who has taken a bath needs washing, he is clean all over . . . .' "

John 13:1-16

Yes, "the cross is still there," especially when we eat and drink the Lord's supper; that meal is always a repast that takes place for us on the water's edge. Baptism admits us to the holy communion, and every time we partake of the Eucharist the gifts we received in holy baptism — the forgiveness of sins, deliverance from the devil, and the promise of eternal life — are renewed. On Holy Thursday, especially, we eat our supper by the water. We know this because the cross takes us there.

Back at the beginning of December a couple of years ago, my wife and I spent several very enjoyable days in San Antonio, Texas, at the annual meeting of a professional society to which I belong, the Academy of Homiletics; it consists entirely of people who teach preaching in theological seminaries all over the country and Canada. One day we went to a late afternoon mass in the Cathedral of San Fernando; it was from the bell tower of this church that Santa Anna's troops were first sighted and a warning signal was given. That church is giving other signals now about the incursion of Mexicans into the United States, in its Mexican/American mass; we were there to "read" some of those contemporary signals. The priest told us that 40 percent of the Roman Catholic baptisms performed in Texas today are in Spanish speaking families. Santa Anna's army was inconsequential in numbers when compared with the contemporary influx of Mexicans into the United States, he seemed to be saying.

After the mass, my wife and I went down to the River Walk to have supper at one of the restaurants bordering the water. We also wanted to see the luminaries, votive candles placed in paper bags on both sides of the narrow river; this was the first of two weekends when the luminaries would be used to usher in the festivities of Advent/Christmas. Indeed, it was beautiful to see, and to hear, too, as people in the large tourist boats spontaneously sang Christmas carols. The sidewalks, which go right up to the edge of the river, were crowded with people. We were lucky enough to get a table right at the water's edge and, I realize now, it was an experience we'll always remember. Later, we joined the crowds and walked on both sides of the river, covering as much of it as we could in that great press of people. There were so many people that I expected to see someone fall into, or be pushed into, that shallow stream. It didn't happen, or, if it did, we didn't see it happen.

There was a more important and unforgettable supper, held in an upper room in Jerusalem 2,000 years ago. It is so memorable that it is repeated in some parts of the Christian church every single day of the year. And on Holy Thursday, practically every Christian church stages the supper that was central to the drama that occurred on that night so long ago.

John's account of that dinner is radically different from those of the other gospel writers and the Apostle Paul; he gives no report of the institution of the Lord's supper, the Eucharist or thanksgiving, as we call it again today. Instead, John tells us about this strange incident that signals the beginning of Jesus' passion and death the next day; he gets up from the meal, removes his outer clothing, takes a towel, and proceeds to wash the disciples' feet.

He took a towel
  That night before the Passover was to begin,
  Stripped off his clothing, filled a basin with
      water —
  And washed his disciples' feet before their
  last supper;

A towel . . .
  ensign of the servant,
  symbol of the slave doomed to a life of menial
      service,
  a kind of living death.

A towel . . .
  so out of character for the Son of Man, the King
      of kings —

A towel . . .
  such a humble act; a step toward the cross.

A towel . . .
  such a lesson —
      "Not my feet only, but also my hands and my head."[14]

Peter resisted; he knew that he should be washing his Lord's feet. To him, it must have been an incongruous act that made about as much sense to him as the prayer of a little boy I know makes to his father. His mother takes him to Sunday church

59

school, and she has taught him to pray. He insists on saying a table grace at every meal, much to the consternation of his father who claims to be an agnostic. He always finishes that prayer with a petition for his father's pack mule, "And God bless Blackie, too." I suspect that the child's very intelligent father can't understand his "Saint Francis-like" prayer at all; I doubt if it is even "cute" to him, but he doesn't do anything to stop his son's "pack mule prayer."

When Jesus washed the disciples' feet, Peter wanted to turn this experience into a kind of baptism, ". . . not my feet only, but my hands and my head as well." He wanted a baptism that was the next thing to total immersion, which some Christians insist is the only valid form of baptism. But the footwashing was more than an act of cleansing; it was the action of a servant, a slave; in Jesus' case, it was the first lesson that the Lord could teach his disciples. He knew that Judas Iscariot was about to betray him; and he believed that his death would soon occur; the time for the fulfillment of the Scriptures was at hand. On the morrow, he realized, he would die.

Loren Eiseley's autobiographical book, *The Night Country*, was written at a time when he realized that his death was not far off. When he was a small boy, his father had taken him out at night and they had watched Halley's Comet blazing its trail across the night sky. He had whispered to the child he held on his shoulder, "It will come back again. You will be an old man then, but you will see it for me."[15] Eisley sensed that he would not live long enough to see the fulfillment of his father's prophecy; he didn't. In one of his posthumously published writings, *The Lost Notebooks of Loren Eiseley,* the original introduction to *The Night Country* is published. In it, Eiseley tells how his grandmother, who, he claims, saved his sanity simply by sitting with him during the long, sleepless night when he became an insomniac after his father died, sensed that her death was near. He writes, "My grandmother, in her declining years, used to stand and whisper at the window. If one drew close, they could hear a kind of dialogue going on between two levels of consciousness, one of the day, one of the night, the two distinctly separated in old age. Finally one morning I saw the lined hawk features working as she stared far away down the street. 'There comes the dead wagon,' I heard her murmur in a dialect of a vanished day . . . .''

He continues the story: "Not long after she died, the 'wagon,' as she had foreseen, drew up in the street. She had penetrated further than I could see with the clear eyes of youth on that cold October morning. Though I stood beside her at the time, I would never have dared ask her to describe her inward seeing. Her eyes were frighteningly remote and she seemed listening, perhaps for hoofbeats sounding in her head."[16] As they reclined at the table that night Jesus might have "heard" the shouts of the crowd at his trial, "Crucify, crucify!" or the blows of the hammer on the nails as they impaled him to the tree on top of that awful hill that actually looked like a skull. That he was aware of his impending death is one thing of which we may be certain. He went "up to Jerusalem" for this.

But Jesus was very much aware of the terrible ordeal that the disciples, too, would go through in the next few days. He washed their feet and asked them if they understood what he was doing; they should become servants of each other, of all people, just as he was showing himself to be a servant. And at the end of this incident he tells them, "A new commandment I give you; that you love one another as I have loved you." In that mass at the San Fernando Cathedral, the priest, Father Vergilio Elizondo, told us, in his sermon, that he had just come from the hospital where he had been visiting a Mexican boy who had been severely injured attempting to enter the United States illegally. On a previous visit, he learned that the boy had literally nothing to his name, so he made an appeal, raised some money and collected a considerable amount of clothing, which he had presented to the boy. During his visit before the mass, he asked the boy where the new clothing was. The boy answered, "I sent it all (including the money) to my brothers in Mexico; they need it more than I do." That's the spirit of loving service that Jesus was attempting to teach his followers "on the night in which he was betrayed." And this is one of the memories revived in reliving the events of that last night before his death in this meal at a table by the water's edge.

We can't possibly fail to remember the significance of this night "before he died," can we? But we just might forget that we are having supper by the water tonight, not the water of River Walk, nor of an old woman whose grandson talks about the "stream of dark and light" separating for him, too, but the water of the font which stands next to the table tonight. It is not there to wash our feet, nor to provide an actual bath for us, but to remind us that we, too, have been washed clean by his sacrifice, and our garments have been bleached in the blood of the Lamb, and, thereby, to renew all of the gifts he bestowed upon us in holy baptism so that we may become loving servants, who are willing and able to sacrifice themselves for others. That's a tall order to fill in a world that constantly tells people to live for themselves above everything else.

Jesus has freed us from our death sentence and has liberated us so that we might live the new life in which we demonstrate to the world that we love one another — love all people — in his holy name. His last supper is our first and foremost supper. The table is set with bread and wine by the water's edge. Come, eat and drink at the table that stands next to the font because this meal reassures us that the cross is still there.

9

Marked At The Cross

"When they reached the place called The Skull, they crucified him there and the two criminals also, one on the right, the other on the left."

Luke 23:33-46

Yes, "the cross is still there;" Jesus' death on Good Friday on that little hill that looked like a skull tells us so. That cross will forever be a sign and symbol of the unmeasurable and undying love that God has for every human being. It really does declare that "God so loved the world that he gave his only-begotten Son" to die for all of us ". . . that the world through him might have life." That is a truth that all of us can cling to regardless of what might happen to us in this life. We were marked for eternal life at the cross of Christ.

Luke compresses the account of Jesus' death into 14 short, but packed, verses of his story about the Lord. Jesus didn't die alone; two criminals were crucified with him, men who had been condemned to death for crimes against society or the state. And Luke reports three "words" that Jesus spoke as he hung upon the cross in the paroxysms of pain and death. What Jesus said tells us what we need to know about him, his mission, and the reality of the realm of eternal life. Good Friday is the day that the good news was written in blood, the blood of Jesus, for all time, for all people to see and to read. That blood can never be washed away and, for that reason, the cross will stand forever and the mark of the cross, made on our foreheads in baptism, can never be erased or removed.

First of all, Jesus said, "Father, forgive them, for they do not know what they are doing." The Romans and the Jewish leaders had no way of knowing that they were participating in the deliverance of humanity that God planned for the world from the beginning of time. But that was what they were doing, weren't they? Jesus had said, "For this I came into the world," and, "I, if I be lifted up will draw all people to myself." This painful and insidious death on the cross was the only way that the world could be saved.

That doesn't seem to say much for God, does it? A genuine God ought to have been able to figure out a better ending to the story, shouldn't he? And a real heavenly Father would hardly allow his "only Son" to die with criminals, would he? But that was really the best that God could do for people; it was the only way that once and for all, humanity could be delivered from sin, death, and the domain of the devil. And it was appropriate and fitting that Jesus should not only die, but die between two criminals, because he had declared, "I have come, not to save the righteous, but sinners." And that means all people, for "all have sinned and fallen short of the kingdom of heaven."

A few years ago, the University of Leeds conducted a religious survey in which they asked several thousands of the people living in England about their faith. They discovered that less than 10 percent of the people go to church with regularity, but that over 70 percent attend worship on festivals, as well as participate in baptisms, weddings, and funerals. Strangely enough, 89 percent of the people surveyed believe in some sort of spiritual power, and 71 percent of the people claimed that they prayed every day. Their prayers were mostly for power to cope with life, to survive from day to day, and, especially, for healing. There was no evidence given to show that they pray for their enemies in the spirit of "Father, forgive," as so many of the English did at the dedication of the new cathedral at Coventry.

Could it be that they and we, too, forget the announced intention of Jesus Christ to save all of the people of the world? He did just that: prayed for the very enemies of God himself when they nailed him to that trunk of a tree with only one "cross-branch" and left him hanging there to die in the heat of the midday sun. They didn't know what they were doing when they condemned and executed Jesus, but they were actually playing into the hands of God and participating in the work of salvation in Jesus' death and resurrection. But we should know this: When we learn to pray for others, in the spirit of Jesus' prayer when he was dying, our prayers are pleasing to God and have really become holy and genuine offerings to the God who loves every single one of us.

Second, as Jesus hung there on the cross, one of the two thieves took up the taunts of the crowd, "He saved others, let him save himself if he is the Christ of God, the Chosen One." The thief cried out, "Save yourself" and added, "and save us as well." What could Jesus be expected to do? The thief didn't really think Jesus could not break loose from the spikes, or he would not have said what he did. He knew that Jesus was helpless to assist him and his companion in any way; all he could do was hang there until he died. But could it be that he was afraid to die even with Jesus?

One of my students told about a minor operation that his son had to have, and how, as they sat in the waiting room at the hospital, watching television, the five-year-old boy said, "Daddy, I'm scared." His father hugged him and wiped a tear from his cheek. "There was little else I could do," he says. When the time came to go to the operating room, both parents walked with him as far as they could, then a nurse took his hand and "he walked down the hallway in those silly hospital pajamas, and as he started to turn a corner he looked back. Still clutching his bears he disappeared." His father remembers, "I stood there, helpless. There was nothing I could do." But, as for Jesus, he wasn't entirely helpless; the other thief perceived that.

That remarkable man, the God-fearing criminal hanging beside Jesus, rebuked the thief who taunted Christ, reminding him that they were getting what they deserved, but that Jesus was innocent and had not earned condemnation and death. And he, in that time of torture and torment, acknowledged the Lordship of Christ with his prayer-request, "Jesus, remember me when you come into your kingdom." Jesus answered, "I promise you, today you will be with me in paradise." If that thief made any reply, it was lost and all we know about his death, according to Luke, is that he hung there until he died, but knowing that God loved him and that Christ had prepared a place for him in the realm of heaven himself. There is no doubt, in my mind, that that word from Jesus "restored his soul."

"It happened," says Melvin Konner, an anthropologist who teaches at Emery University in Atlanta, "before the transformation, before he (Jesse Jackson) was a major force of presidential politics, before he had kissed thousands of white babies. My brother, Larry, and I were on the eighth floor of the Cedars-Sinai Medical Center, in Los Angeles, a place we had left only rarely in the preceding two weeks." They were there because Larry's 44-year-old wife was in a near-comatose state following surgery to remove a blood clot in her brain stem. As they sat near the elevator, a group of men emerged from the elevator, and Melvin and his brother realized that the man leading the procession was Jesse Jackson. He reached across a low table and shook hands with him and Melvin told him, "Don't worry, Jesse. You've got a whole family of liberals here." "Get their cards," Jesse directed an aide, who took Melvin's business card. The group moved off quickly and Larry mused, "He must be visiting Bill Cosby's mother . . . . Do you think I could get him to visit Ronnie, say a prayer for her?'' Melvin explains, ''Between one atheist and another this suggestion made an odd but apt sort of sense. We had reason to hope that Ronnie would know what was happening, and we knew that if she did, she would love it. As for the effect on the morale of everyone on the floor — everyone involved in her care — it could be incalculable. 'Ask him,' Melvin urged Larry, 'What do you have to lose?' ''

"Excuse me, Rev. Jackson," (Larry) my brother said. ''My wife's in intensive care, she may not make it. I was wondering if you could stop in and see her for a minute. Maybe say a prayer. It would mean a lot to her. And to the family.'' Jackson asked, ''What's wrong with her?'' without breaking his stride, ''and a series of rapid, gentle questions from Jackson produced her name, facts about the children, her career and more. The knot of men, us included, moved straight past the elevators without slowing down. 'We can't do this,' said an aide to another. 'It's the only plane today.' '' But they did, and when they got to the intensive care unit, Jesse Jackson "pulled on the door handle. He had never hesitated or slowed down. My brother said, 'We can't go in with all these people.' 'Just my son,' said Jackson. He entered and swept past the nurse's station to Ronnie's bed. He went to her right side, which he had learned was the better one. 'Ronnie, it's Jesse Jackson. Take my hand, Ronnie.' ''

He took her hand, formed a circle with Ronnie's sister, Larry, the nurse, and Jackson's son and ''then spoke directly to a presence that at least he felt clearly: 'Lord, you're the God that parted the Red Sea, the God that helped Daniel in the den.' He mentioned only Old Testament miracles — this was, after all, a Jewish hospital. 'We need a miracle. Touch this room. Touch this woman. Give strength to the family.' By the time he said 'Amen,' my brother (Larry) was sobbing loudly. As he pronounced that word, Ronnie opened her eyes. It was not unusual, but the timing was remarkable. The circle broke up, but Jackson did not leave. He took my brother in his large, strong arms and held him until he stopped crying. That was all.

It took only a few minutes. But what we could not stop talking about later was not what he had done but how he had done it . . . Many weeks later, after she had recovered her speech, Ronnie told the story of the visit over and over again. 'Jesse Jackson came to see me,' she was delighted to tell visitors.''[17] For nearly 2,000 years, people have been telling the story of Jesus and how he said to the repentant thief, "I promise you . . . Paradise." The thief never had a chance to tell the world of Jesus' promise to him, but we tell it because the story applies to us and all who recognize their sinfulness and pray, "Remember me . . . forgive me, O Lord." He does. The cross assures us of that.

Third, shortly after this exchange, Jesus died, but only after he had said, "Father, into your hands I commit my spirit." His work was completed, his pain and suffering were at an end, and the "time of his departure was at hand"; Jesus knew that all was well and that he was returning to the Father who had sent him to redeem the world. Another of my students tells how she visited her grandfather's farm with her family when she was a little girl. Her grandfather asked if she could stay a few days after her parents went home; she could and did. Her father had said, "Now be a good girl, Barbara, and I will be waiting for you on Friday when they stop the train to let you off at the crossing west of our farm."

When the time came for her to return home, her grandfather took her to the train, gave the conductor her ticket and told him where she was going. Her grandfather asked, "You aren't afraid, are you?" Barbara answered, "No. Well, maybe just a little, because I've never been on a train before. But then I just remember that Daddy promised he would be waiting for me, and I know he will be standing right there when I get off." She said, "That was all the assurance I needed." And that's how it was when the train slowed down and stopped near the country road. Barbara said, "I stepped down from the train into daddy's waiting arms."

There's something of that in Jesus' last words, "Father, into your hands I commit my spirit." Jesus had been in perfect communion and harmony with God all of his life, therefore, he could face death knowing that his heavenly Father was waiting to receive him. And that same knowledge makes it possible for us to face all that there is in life confident that in all things, and especially when time runs out on us and we face death. Our heavenly Father, who supports us in every one of life's situations, will greet us with open arms when this life comes to a close.

Many years ago, Dr. Howard Hageman published a book of sermons under the title, *They Called This Friday Good.* In the awful death that Jesus suffered that first Good Friday — the "bad" thing that happened to Jesus — something very good occurred for us: Our salvation was accomplished, eternal life was promised to all, and death became a return to the Father who created us in the first place. The cross, whose mark was made on our foreheads in baptism, assures us of that. Yes, the cross is still there. It always will be.

10

Marked In An Empty Tomb —
The Cross Is Still There

"The other women with them (Mary Magdala, Joanna, and Mary, the Mother of James) also told the apostles (about their experience at the Tomb), but this story of theirs seemed pure nonsense, and they did not believe them."   Luke 24:11

Yes, the cross is still there upon our foreheads and in our hearts. Easter, more than anything else, assures us of that. Because we believe in both Jesus' death and resurrection, we declare: "Christ is risen! He is risen indeed!" Our Lord's resurrection is at the heart of the Christian faith. Without the reality of the resurrection, the cross would be nonsense, Jesus would be a well-intentioned martyr, and the Christian church simply would not exist. He died, but he is alive forever! We have been marked by the cross at Easter for time and eternity.

On that first Easter Day, when the women told the disciples what had happened at the tomb of Jesus, their story

71

was too incredible for the disciples to believe. They knew that Jesus was dead, and that people just don't rise from the grave, especially after someone had been dead for most of three days; such things don't even occur in our time when miracles of resuscitation commonly take place. The news was preposterous; it was just too much to believe. Like most people who had lived before them, and many people who have lived since the first century A.D., the thought of a person overcoming death — resurrection — was "an idle tale," pure nonsense.

Toward the end of the third week after Easter a couple of years ago, local newspaper headlines announced: "Come hell or high water, atheists set for conclave." The national convention of American Atheists was held in Minneapolis, Minnesota, a state wherein 95 percent of the people claim to believe in some sort of god and more than half of the population is supposed to attend church every week. It seemed ludicrous that the atheists would meet in this city but, apparently, they wanted to make known their "beliefs" to the people who worship the God of the Jews and Christians; they simply can't accept the biblical account of creation or the other stories of how God deals with people here on earth.

One woman, Cora Wheeler, was interviewed, apparently because she was a rather typical atheist. She told the reporter that her father was an atheist, but that he never used the term. Her mother sent her to Sunday School, but "her father would always point out the 'fantasies' in the various Bible stories in those Sunday sessions." She didn't realize that she was an atheist until she was an adult: "I was sorting mail at my job at the post office and saw a copy of the magazine, *American Atheist,* and I said, 'So that's what I am.' " She believes that if she would ever wind up before the judgment seat of God, she'll have two questions: "I'll ask how come (this deity) gave me a brain to think with and why has he or she been so hidden. Nobody asks you to believe in trees. They don't require belief. They can be seen . . . . Religion came from primitive times. For early Christians, God was a man sitting up in the clouds. Then they learned about space. So the church, to save the faith, made it a spiritual God, invisible. It's obviously made up."[18] For her and the others, the resurrection of the Son of God can be nothing else except pure and unadulterated nonsense.

So much for the resurrection of Jesus if we stop reading the story at the point where the disciples regard it as "an idle tale." But Peter, at least, was curious and ran out to the tomb to see if it really was empty; the two angels were gone but the cloths in which Jesus had been wrapped so hurriedly on the day he died were there. He was amazed, but he still didn't believe the story. Nor did Cleopas and the "other disciple" accept the possibility of Jesus' rising from the dead as they walked toward Emmaus that same evening; they were still wondering why he had to die on a cross, why he had to die at all. Christ joined them and said to them, when he heard what they were talking about, "You foolish men! So slow to believe the full message of the prophets! Was it not ordained that the Christ should suffer and so enter into his glory?" He had to review the prophecies about himself with them, but it was only when he broke the bread at dinner that they recognized him, "and he vanished out of their sight."

In the case of Peter and the others, it wasn't until Jesus appeared to them in a locked room that the issue of his resurrection was addressed and settled once and for all time, at least, for them. Jesus spoke, "Peace be with you!" Luke tells us that they thought they were seeing a ghost, but the Lord asked, "Why are you so agitated, and why are these doubts rising in your hearts? Look at my hands and feet; yes, it is I indeed. Touch me and see for yourselves; a ghost has no flesh and bones as you can see I have." Even when he showed them his hands and feet, Luke tells us, "their joy was so great that they still could not believe it, and they stood there dumbfounded." To prove he was real and no ghost, Jesus took some fish and ate it "before their eyes." At last, they believed that the Lord had risen as he said he would, and they soon were ready to go out into all the world with the good news, "He is risen, as he said. He is risen indeed!"

Easter assures us that Jesus did not die in vain upon the cross at Calvary; his death served God's purpose, which was to reconcile the world to himself through the death of Jesus Christ. His resurrection reminds us that God accomplished his intention, despite the unfathomable mystery that will always surround his death and resurrection. The cross remains both a visible and invisible symbol of the faith. The resurrection holds it up for the world to see and to know that this is the sign of God's love for humanity. The cross declares to the world, "God loves the world so much that he has done everything he can to save those whom he has created in his image." The "empty" cross announces to the world that God is not only alive, but he has an active interest in the affairs of his people and does all he can to assure them that he, God the Father, is still God and has ultimate control over heaven and earth. The Lord is still alive!

When a colleague, Dr. James Limburg, was in East Germany several years ago, he met the pastor of a church in a small town near Dresden. He discovered that the man was a musician (Jim is too; he plays a trombone), plays a trumpet; he has played it in the brass band of his church for more than 50 years. Jim asked him, "Do you have your trumpet with you?" Indeed he did; he brought out a battered old horn and they went out into the garden behind the home where they had met, and he played a couple of hymns, as he does at home in his parish. He told Jim that no public religous activities were permitted in his town, and that his parsonage was right across the street from the city hall. Every morning, promptly at 8 a.m., as the government workers begin their day, he opens a window facing that building and plays two hymns appointed for the day. It is probably an illegal act, but he has done it for years and no one has bothered him. Prof. Limburg asks, "Why does he do it? Simply this: to keep the memory of God alive in that little town." That's really what the cross does in our world, isn't it? But it really does more than that; it reminds us that God is not only alive but that, in due time, our living and ever-present Lord will actually return to usher in the fullness of the kingdom of God and the era when he will rule "forever and ever."

As for us, we have the opportunity to meet that risen Lord, especially when we receive the Body and Blood in that holy supper which he prepared for us. And he comes to us and allows us to "touch" him by taking the elements in our hands and eating and drinking what he gives us. And when we do that, the invisible, indelible, and illuminated mark of the cross that was traced on our foreheads in baptism assures us that he is alive, that his death has delivered us from sin and death, and that through our baptism we participate, not only in his death but also in the benefits of his resurrection.

A couple of days after Easter a few years ago, an 18-year-old woman who had been baptized as a baby in our church was beaten and murdered by several young men; her name was Mollie Larson. In his sermon at her funeral, Pastor Paul K. Peterson said: "We are gathered in this room where some of you have been before. In our vault back in the office there is a book that tells us that on January 31, 1971, Mollie Michelle was here in this room, and in this room she was baptized in the name of the Father and of the Son and of the Holy Spirit. In that simple washing and those few words God made a promise to Mollie. God established a no-strings covenant with Mollie that was contingent not on Mollie, not on Mollie's parents or family or friends. It was not a two-way promise to which she was bound to conform with some established pattern of behavior. God simply said to Mollie, 'I am going to be your God. I am going to hold you close to my heart, and nothing, nothing will ever change that.' God is not into going back on his promises. He makes them and they stick. The apostle says it so well in this lesson (Romans 8:31-39), 'I am sure . . . that neither death, nor life, nor angels, nor principalities , nor things present, nor things to come, nor powers, nor height, nor depth, nor anything else in all creation, will be able to separate us from the love of God in Christ Jesus our Lord.' "

Pastor Peterson added: "If we get that promise straight and riveted in our head and heart, then we might find ourselves with more questions than we had before. Chief among them might be, Then where was God on that dark night, on that godforsaken highway? Clearly God wasn't around to throw a protective shield around Mollie when she needed it. That's true . . . . The only answer that can satisfy our longing for understanding is to say once again, I am sure . . . I am sure that God was where the world needs him to be, on the cross at work for our redemption. And at the moment the blows fell that destroyed this young life, the man on the cross was the first to weep, just as he has wept for all of us who stray, who are overwhelmed by circumstances that defy understanding, and he weeps with us for all our losses, too. God's good purpose, God's will, is not for death. That's what Easter really means. God's purpose is to give us life, and give it to us abundantly. And we are here to say today, even through our tears, this is God's will for Mollie." And he adds, "That's the promise God made to Mollie back those few years ago in this room . . . (and) that life is God's gift now fulfilled in ways that pass our understanding today."[19] For Mollie — for all of us who have been baptized in the name of the Father and of the Son and of the Holy Spirit — Easter declares, "The cross is still there."

Outside of the downtown hotels during the convention of American Atheists, I saw a car with special Minnesota license plates upon it. There were no numbers, only letters which spelled out "ATHEIST." The owner of the car wanted the world to know that he or she could not believe in God; it was a way of announcing to the world that as far as this person was concerned, God is dead. But we believe that God is very much alive. And we believe that God not only exists, but that he loves us and has given us proof of that love in the death and resurrection of our Lord, Jesus Christ. So we take our God-given faith into the world, proclaiming to all, "Christ is risen. He is risen indeed." And we believe that the cross, the sign of God's incomprehensible and immeasurable love, is still there and always will be on our foreheads. Yes, the cross is still there because the crucified Christ is alive forever!

Notes

1. *Lutheran Book of Worship*, p. 124.

2. Wayne B. Robinson, editor. *Journeys Toward Narrative Preaching*. New York: Pilgrim Press, 1990, p. 64.

3. Edmund A. Steimle. *Disturbed By Joy*. Philadelphia: Fortress, 1967, p. 95.

4. Leslie D. Weatherhead. *Key Next Door*. New York: Abingdon, 1960, p. 95.

5. Neville Clark. *Interpreting The Resurrection*. Philadelphia: Westminster, 1967, p. 108.

6. Barbara Schmick. "The Catechesis of the Good Shepherd," in *Liturgy,* Volume 8, Number 2.

7. George Buttrick. *Sermons Preached In A University Church*. New York: Abingdon, 1959, p. 164.

8. Minneapolis *Star Tribune,* August 12, 1990.

9. Read, also, James S. Stewart's sermon, "The Darkness Where God Was," in *The Wind Of The Spirit*. New York: Abingdon, 1968.

10. Minneapolis *Star Tribune,* July 8, 1990.

11. Originally published in the Los Angeles *Times.*

12. Read Gerard Sloyan's "What Is Liturgical Preaching?" in *Liturgy*, Volume 8, Number 2, as well as some of his meditations (for example, *Nothing Of Yesterday Preaches*).

13. From the Minneapolis *Star Tribune,* 1989.

14. Excerpts from my sermon, "He Took a Towel," in *Augsburg Sermons,* Gospels, Series A, 1974.

15. See Eiseley's *The Invisible Pyramid* for his story "The Star Dragon." Scribner's: New York, 1970.

16. See, also, *The Lost Notebooks of Loren Eiseley*. Boston: Little, Brown & Co., 1987.

17. This story was reprinted in the Minneapolis *Star Tribune*.

18. From the Minneapolis *Star Tribune*, August, 1988.